WHERE I WAS BORN

POEMS

WHERE I WAS BORN

By

IKEOGU OKE

FOURTH DIMENSION PUBLISHING CO. LTD,
ENUGU

First published in 2003 by
FOURTH DIMENSION PUBLISHING CO., LTD
16 Fifth Avenue, City Layout, P.M.B. 01164, Enugu, Nigeria.
Tel: +234 42 459969. Fax: +234 42 456904.
Email: info@fdpbooks.com, fdpbooks@aol.com
Website: http://www.fdpbooks.com

© Ikeogu Oke 2003

ISBN 978 158 499 7

CONDITIONS OF SALE

All rights reserved. No part of this publication may be reproduced, stored in a retrieval system, or transmitted in any form or by any means, electronic, mechanical, photocopying, recording, or otherwise without the prior permission of the publisher.

Photoset in Nigeria by Fourth Dimension Publishers, Enugu, and printed in the United Kingdom by Lightning Source UK Ltd.

Contents	Page
Dedication	ix
Requiem, Not Requiem	ix
Acknowledgments	xi
Introduction	xiii
Preface	xvii
The Way I Want To Go	3
Resolutions	4
Carcady	5
Self Reliance?	6
Crossroads	7
A Late Devotion	8
Thus Says the Gadfly	9
A Poet's Prayer	10
Rural Dwellers	15
Where I Was Born	16
Dialogue of Self and Country	18
Solidarity	20
The Rubric	23
Athlete	27
Gani Fawehinmi	28
The Handout	30
To Fidel	31
A Year After	32
Dawn of Democide	33
The Scapegoat	35
Emissary	39
To a Sparrow	40
The Chicks	41
Euthanasia	42
Apologia	43
To a Murdered Egret	44
To an Injured Rat	45
The Question	46
Pandrillus	48
Child of Man	50
Weep Not, Child	51

Uyi – My Boyhood's Last Love	55
Lyric for Uyi (I)	56
Lyric for Uyi (II)	57
Lucky Rose	58
Serenade	59
Omen	60
A Nuptial Flight	61
The Receptionist	62
Departure	63
Girl in My Class	64
The Dance	65
Song: To IJ	66
Call Her Belinda	67
Love	69
A New Deal	70
Dirge	72
On the Pulse of the Millennium	75
The Challenger	77
Indictments	78
Reminiscence	79
Jolly side Exchange	80
Little women; little girls	81
Thoughts by Sky and Sea	82
Tournament in Jebba	83
Mutual Props	84
A Stellar Monologue	85
Interrogation	86
A Clown's Toast	87
A Lunatic in the Library	88
Cradle Song	90
I Heard You Were Stabbed	91
Free Among These Hills	92
Spirit of the Age?	93
Nocturne	95
Tropical Facts	96
The Passage	98
Metaphors	101
It Was His Doubts	102

After Chrysalis	103
The Preacher and the Voice	107

To the memory of my Father, Oke Kalu,
and of Victor Nwankwo[1]

REQUIEM, NOT REQUIEM

(To Victor Nwankwo)

The fear of death does not make a Methuselah,
Nor does the love of life or its taking.
And those who sought to shoot down your star
Have found their aim unworthy, their goal mistaken.
They struck the hole at the core of futility
Where strife, wind and despair pass to nothingness.
Theirs are crumbled hopes built on credulity,
Ours a faith that shall not waver, nor depress.
Yet our radiant, curved paths meet and part
And meet again on realms distant from their kind
As their dim caves are distant from your luminous sky:
Those who build in the heart live in the heart.
Those who build in the mind live in the mind.
And though they pass on, they never die.

November 28, 2002

---

[1] The Managing Director of Fourth Dimension Publishers, Enugu, and the founding Chairman of African Publishers Network (APNET): assassinated in Enugu, in south eastern Nigeria, on August 29, 2002.

ACKNOWLEDGEMENTS

Every work in this volume is definitive and, where applicable, supersedes any other extant version. I am grateful to Ben Griffiths and Faber and Faber Ltd for the permission to reprint extracts of three lines from Seamus Heaney's "Station Island" and four lines from W. H. Auden's "The Shield of Achilles" as epigraphs to "The Way I Want To Go" and "Solidarity" respectively. I also owe debts of gratitude to Nkemakolam Udo, Donna L. Miesbach, Ngwobia (Chubby) Ibem, Paddy Ezeala, Samuel Oyongha, Emma Egwuonwu, Essien Etukudo, Bam Efoli, Mesembe Edet, Steve O. Ikpa, U. T. Moneme, and Dr. Angrey Unimna, friends whose encouragement I have counted on through the years. "Tournament in Jebba" was first published in *The Nigerian Chronicle*, "The Handout" in the Post Express Literary Series (PELS) and "The Way I Want To Go" in *Gleanings, A Bi Monthly Discussion of Life Issues*. "The Question" was commissioned by The Nigerian Conservation Foundation for the occasion of her Annual Dinner Dance of 6th November 1999 and read at the event held in the Banquet Hall of Le Meridien Eko Hotel, Lagos. "On the Pulse of the Millennium" was written on the special request of Mr. Hilliard Etta and read at the Millennium Dinner of the Calabar Municipal Council held on 2nd January 2000 at Marian Hotels, Calabar. It was first published in *The Defender* as "On the Pulse of the Nation" (an editorially re titled and abridged version) by courtesy of Etubom Bassey Ekpo Bassey. I am equally grateful to these other individuals and institutions for their patronage, and for the moral support of my mother, Eresi, and my siblings (Kalu, Ada, John, Ogbonne, Oluchi), and to Rev. Amos N. Kalu, Dr. Edet Ikpi, Dr. Eka Williams, Dr. Julius N. Ogu, Dr. Kalu Ojah, Prof. Ebele Eko and Prof. E. M. Uka, for years of sterling support.

I.O.

INTRODUCTION

Where I Was Born is dominated by a desire to produce poetry that is marked by directness and simplicity of thought and diction but does not lose touch with profundity, elegance, and, perhaps, sublimity and grandeur.

In compiling it I have not been unconscious of the ideological turn of mind among certain poets and critics of African origin that, to qualify as African and communicate African values effectively, an African poet may not be expected to draw on presumably non African resources of form like rhyme which, incidentally, has had a rather extensive presence in my work, though I come from an African background. Certain sensibilities implicated in an inclination to rhyming – to paraphrase some of such poets and critics – are colonialist. And so, to "decolonise" our literature, they urge us to eschew all such sensibilities and literary techniques whose use could suggest a neo colonialist capitulation to the forces of literary imperialism. To that, let it suffice to say, in the interim, that writers will do well to realize that, as individuals, they accept to surrender their claim to the prerogative of innovation at their own peril and to the detriment of their progress as artists.

For all the similarities of theme and style that pervade African literature by the assessment of some of its critics and analysts, a closer observation would reveal that no two African writers ply their craft alike; and that so far our writers' interpretations of our continent have – in a healthy, non derogatory sense – been the creative equivalent of the blind men trying to make sense of the elephant in a well known fable. They more often than not reflect as many shades of interpretation as there are angles of contact or perception.

In effect, the African poet (or writer) is essentially an individual whose works reveal that in literature, as in other departments of art, reality is not infrequently coloured by the artist's own unique perspective – and that in that scheme of colouration the hues of idiosyncrasy are never quite left out.

And whether or not an African poet may adopt any verse form – regardless of whether it is classified as "rhymed", "free", "bound", "local", "foreign", "avant garde", and so forth – and in doing so still communicate African values effectively – should sensibly be a matter for choice and ability on the part of the poet, rather than be decided through the canonical prescriptions of critics and literary theorists. Down the ages bad poems have been written in practically every literary form known to man. And I do not see that there is a strict relationship between a poem's form and its intrinsic quality as a rhythmic filtering of experience through the prism of imagination.

Indeed I am of the view that African values, and no less the African experience, can be clothed in any poetic garment regarding form. And whether the hem of the garment were left frayed (as in free verse) or sewn up (as in rhyme) should be far less important to the liberal critic than the appropriateness of such clothing. That is, the consideration of how successfully the poet has utilized the form (in question) in a compositional context.

In the following lines from "The Rubric", for instance, I simply adapted an Igbo[2] idiomatic expression. (And a people's values, I believe, can be gleaned from such expressions). I then modified the expression to blend with a related English idiomatic expression[3], and subjected the mixture to a rhyme scheme and to the demands of a compositional situation aimed at urging a desperate sense of urgency on the reader. Thus:

> Like prudent herds, not given to delay,
> Strive to find the dark goat while it's day,
> Thus we must strive, and
> Striving chase the thief of time away,
> Lest the day should waste upon our hand.

Therefore a liberal attitude to form – or any other index of eclecticism – need not obviate a poet's consciousness of his (or her) roots.

The poems are grouped into five loose categories under subtitles beginning with **Scarab on the Shelf** and terminating with **Appendix**, while poems under **Where I Was Born, These I Have Loved, Sheaves of Passion** and **Omnibus**

---

[2] The Igbo (also Ibo) are indigenous to South eastern Nigeria.
[3] Idiomatic expression(s): i. *Ana eji ehihie acho ewu ojii* (Igbo): "A dark goat is searched for by daytime" is a rough translation. The meaning has affinity with that of "Make hay while the sun shines" (English). ii. Procrastination is the thief of time (English).

fill the interlude. Incidentally, this arrangement excludes "Preface", whose tenor, I think, commends it to the rather strategic *manifesto* positioning it has, and "Requiem, Not Requiem", which forms part of the dedication.

The poems under **Scarab on the Shelf** hint at the autobiography of a mind fraught with that species of angst that everywhere affects people the path of whose faith and resolve are not infrequently traversed by doubt, as exemplified by the sharp thematic contrast between "Resolutions" and "Crossroads". Under **Where I Was Born** are poems that, to varying degrees, are products of my reflections on my country, and on the larger world, whose pact with despair is sometimes redeemed by the presence of such reformist pillars of hope that inspired "Athlete" and "Gani Fawehinmi". The poems under **These I Have Loved**, most exemplarily "The Chicks" and "Euthanasia", are linked together more or less by a humane affinity with nature and such circumstantial mortal victims portrayed in "Child of Man" and "Weep Not, Child". Most of the poems under **Sheaves of Passion** are, in the main, products of my efforts at the lyrical preservation of cherished romantic attachments, with all their rapture and transiency. Under **Omnibus** are poems that can be described as a miscellaneous bunch, as the subtitle suggests; and, lastly, under **Appendix**, is "The Preacher and the Voice", which, drawing on one of the more famous Biblical legends, portrays a symbolic conflict between freewill and predestination.

Ikeogu Oke
Calabar,
December 2002

PREFACE

Simple is the mission of this muse:
to tune the lyre of an art in use,
cure it of its jangling malady,
and give it back the health of melody.

SCARAB ON THE SHELF

THE WAY I WANT TO GO

> What you do you must do on your own.
> The main thing is to write
> for the joy of it.
>
>   – Seamus Heaney: From "Station Island"

Father has called and warned me not to go
The way I want to go:
"It is no life you spend among the trees!"
Mother as everyone at home agrees.
And good opinion says the trend of the era shows
That those whose pen must feed must write in prose.
"To write in verse," they say, "is agony.
For poets," they press, "do not make money."

And I have given thought to what they say,
While alone and headed on my way.
The wisdom of the world and age apart,
The truly wise must listen to his heart.
And yet the poet should not deny his pain,
Or fail for lack to stress his fair bargain.
For if poets do not make money,
Then, neither does money make poets.

RESOLUTIONS

(On My Twenty first Birthday)

I now can feel that I am freed
From the subtle chains of creed,
And great padlocks that dogma hung
Upon my boyhood eyes and tongue.

I now assume to rule my mind:
From narrow doctrines disinclined;
To be a man in quest of Truth,
From this concrete base of youth.

Everything I'm bound to know;
To know all I must grow,
And sink to hell my curious roots
To send skywards my shoots.

To live for virtue with my soul
Shall be my sole true goal,
Until I breathe my mortal last
Like great minds of the past.

CARCADY

It was raised for virtue and for truth,
a land that boasts the mind's perpetual youth:
where the true and saintly sages rule,
and justice is the crown and royal tool.

It's a high and Spartan land of old,
where the mind is truly free and bold;
where no sovereign bellows with a cane,
and life is ordered, simple, and humane.

There I shall arise and go in haste,
where time is null, so there's none to waste,
and live among the souls in learned bliss,
there, to give my willing thoughts release.

I shall browse among her green leafed books
and lap up nature coursing in her brooks.
I shall have a mansion for my thrills
and clasp the Muses on her verdant hills.

O how each day, amid the public surge,
I hear my kind and thoughtful master urge:
"Arise, poet divine, dare and dare to rise!
The glorious path is paved with sacrifice.
In death, the buried gift is not forgiven.
What life! The life that's not returned as given?
Rise now! Ease the moorings! Make your vessel free!
Set sail for the land of Carcady!"

SELF RELIANCE?

Is he true and truly praised
Whose little haven is raised
   Up by his hands alone?
Who thrives away from strife?
And in the ship of life
   Steers himself alone?

Great? Who hides in nooks
And writes his own books?
   Who explores every region
Of his own mind? Whose thought
Inclines to bring the gods to nought
   And confound religion?

Blessed? Who rests
Upon his own harvests
   Of plenty wheat and corn?
Who works to raise own food
And claims his livelihood
   By his strength alone?

Happy? Such a man
Who must build a barn
   That's truly all his own?
Who must revive his farm,
And even make his jam,
   By himself – alone?

That whose whole garden
Is walled away in hiding,
   Whose every seed
Must sprout in solitude,
Is it, though good,
   A life to be envied?

CROSSROADS

The nadir up above my head,
The zenith down below,
Which, dear master, up or down,
Is the way to go?

Upon my left the narrow way,
Upon my right the wide,
Say, dear master, where the rock
Cleaves for me to hide?

To romp without for mirth and joy,
Or muse within for light,
Master, tell your baffled child,
Which is wrong or right?

My last true friend has joined the crowd
To find his life "some role".
But can he be that fails to solve
Such puzzles of the soul?

A LATE DEVOTION

Father, you went without a goodbye
And left a gaping hollow in our sky.
Death came calling too soon
And caught us napping in the afternoon.

It is true, I must confess,
That while you lived I loved you less.
But now I am almost done for breath,
Grieved by your death.

I have done my penance
With a tearful heart and countenance.
O, to know you are kind to forgive
Him by whom your memory shall live.

And while the river of my life shall run,
And distant heaven keep a distant sun,
And the future trail behind the past,
So long my grief shall last.

Thus Says the Gadfly

It's not in caution that man's safety lies
Or in timid silence when he ought to speak.
An end awaits the valiant as the weak.
Even the dumb dies.

So do not, in your hubris or mistake,
Expect to gag me though I writhe in pain.
"Remove your yoke on me and other men!"
I'll scream it, though you hush me to the stake.

A POET'S PRAYER

When great poets shall meet in heaven
and count their blessings one and even,
Lord, may I be one among their number,
to work with them and play and slumber.

May I sing among The Choir,
groomed by Homer, led by Pindar,
there, before your golden throne,
where my little soul had grown.

May I work as well with Virgil,
tending flocks, or leading vigil
that'll last a night in glorious heaven,
when my wrongs are all forgiven.

Grant me grace to embrace Chaucer:
moral soul and country courser;
sometimes – to lend him some great tales
to tell his audience in the vales.

With Dante, Poe and Baudelaire,
let me share a passion there:
to seek – and guide them up above –
the lost – towards your grace and love.

Bless me too to work with Pushkin:
suited for both sock and buskin,
sated with the draught – serene –
from the spring – at Hippocrene.

And may I – hand in hand with Goethe –
waddle by the streams for health:

sharing memories with each other
from lives we lived for you – our Father.

May I – as well – with Yeats – be found:
flexing friendly wits – profound;
snoozing in libraries: dreaming daydreams,
of bevies crouched by mumbling streams.

And Lord you know of Walt Whitman:
the poet who loved the common man.
I'll love to help him weed the passes,
when I'll need to think in verses.

And sad Neruda – troubled more
for earth and all her hapless poor –
I'll then be blessed to assume a role
to calm his good, unquiet soul.

And Lord, that saint you call "Tagore!
Sweet sage of the mystic lore!"
I'll yet savour from feast to feast
his sumptuous wisdom from the East.

And all true poets too great for mention,
nameless, though of great devotion,
dear Lord, grant them all a place,
by the justice of your grace.

Grant them all a place in heaven,
where your own shall all be even,
who – for all that fame can yield! –
did not reap at all – afield.

And dear Lord by each eventide,
when you take a pleasure ride,
may I – beside your chariot car –
fly a flag for Africa.

WHERE I WAS BORN

RURAL DWELLERS

Rickety rackety are their roads,
More crooked than thievery.
Like torture their travelling modes,
Though their skies are silvery.

And though "they're near to nature's heart
For the springs and woods they have".
But they cannot hold her dear,
Dumped in society's grave.

All their men are bent with toil.
Their youths are hoarier than sentient.
Their women: though so gaunt and frail,
Their weary souls remain patient.

Yes, I see, they're suffering, true!
Though our ruler boasts and says:
"How true that they're dying too!
I've bequeathed their sunniest days."

WHERE I WAS BORN

I

Green hills roll down the slopes to the valley.
The dew is thick at morn.
The birds, each morning, call a tuneful rally,
Where I was born.

Four thousand fountains irrigate the land,
A thousand streams or more.
And nature, with her callous rural hand,
Fills our barnyard store.

Yes. We're a hardy, warrior Igbo people,
Glad yokels to the death.
The earth and folk are one like stream and ripple,
In the land of my birth.

In Akanu Ohafia, the proud sun rises still,
Joyful in its youth's iridescence!
Though the men of lucre test their will
To spoil our innocence.

II

Here the Ezize,
primordial stream,
falls in roaring cascades
down her rocks, clothed
in a shroud of mist
and leaves.

It is the land of the Ikpirikpe Ogu,
dance of men and spirits, spirits
of our fierce ancestral dead, twice
as warlike in the great beyond.

Here the turf
in which my father lies:
calloused to the bones
by grating toil, and yet
was dead for want
and lack of care.

... and the yawning tomb
of minstrelsy, of tales
by moonlight
and the glowing hearth!

High above the crows
are meeting still.
They spiral up
a lucent blue of sky.

...here the land
where... of a sudden
a storm gathers, a dense cumulus
hangs above our heads,
will it crash on us
or drift away?

DIALOGUE OF SELF AND COUNTRY

I have had to go by mid September
with more to forget and less to remember.
Out in the dark and at sea
the vessel I await approaches.

Soon I shall embark,
a lonely sailor on a lonely bark.
Far and near other shores beckon me
to a welcome service and activity.

If the land of our fathers
stabs us like adders
are we still obliged to love it,
to nod our assent to its blind conceit,
and cultivate patriotism
in a loveless acre
massed with rocks?

I was fed up with faith and devotion
that paid back with drudgery and persecution.
Though if you worked in the NEPA
you ran the risk of being known like a leper.
You were the spittoon of your neighbourhood:
you scourged the public for a livelihood!

We breathed corruption.
It coursed through the veins
and arteries of our being.
It enlivened our blood,
like haemoglobin.

And those who plugged their noses
had to go, like this one – retired at 33!

Reformers came to set things right
but laid off the guards
to safeguard the thieves,
and the other who was
part of the old brigade,
they judged us earthlings
from their alien skies, and so
unleashed a scourge of ironies.

Now in the manner of an ill bred dog
the NEPA sniffles at its fresh vomit,
poised to take back slops
it's just disgorged.

But I have some cinder spread on ice.
The ice is glowing and the cinder dies.
Incandescent cubes, smouldering coals,
that inflame and extinguish my goals.
Such my temper that I burn and cool,
the paradox of passions that I rule.

SOLIDARITY

(To The Rt. Hon. Dr. Chuba Okadigbo[1])

That girls are raped, that two boys knife a third,
Were axioms to him, who'd never heard
Of any world where promises were kept,
Or one could weep because another wept.

– W. H. Auden: From "The Shield of Achilles"

In their desperate ways some kings are sure
To invoke corruption to besmear the pure.

Yes a little storm had been brewing.
But more to the point there was also
A desperate logger at work. And we could
Hear his padded footsteps, far as we were
From the heart of the forest.

Then of a sudden a great noise comes
Crashing out with cheers rising to the sky
That the stubborn tree has fallen! Yes, the dreaded
Tree that is also a great tree! Oh fallen, has it?
"The Fall of Okadigbo"[2] is a malapropism.
To be pulled down is not to fall.

To those in search of a circus and not character
Humility was at issue. But why act humble
When your mind is great, and play sweet midget

---

[1] Nigeria's former Senate President, and a strong advocate of separation of powers, controversially impeached on August 8, 2000.
[2] As on the cover of *TELL* magazine of August 14, 2000.

Though you're six feet tall? Just why?
To massage egos and fatuities? To what end?
Those who cry "the soul that sinneth shall die"
Must also urge us to reach for the log in our own eye.
And for those who will savour the unripe fruits
        of vindication:
If one man could pass from prisoner to President,
        then another can.

But why use the same axe we had whined about
To hack at another? – The axe of blackmail
        and of grinning cant!
Is this the human face about which we spoke?
Has change not left us farther down the slope?

Perhaps you should have let the Jumbo Jet fly,
To browse among our herd of sacred cows.
Then the pump price, you should have allowed it
        doubled,
And – just like everyone – played out
        on that public holiday.
You should have praised the loan we do not need.
Then you would have remained our proper saint: tall,
Resplendent in purity, and magnificent.
And a few years hence we shall have
Crowned you Chancellor – in gratitude!

O, stubborn light!
They could not even hide you
Under a bushel: the princes
Of a land of hypocrites.
And all their effort was to mock
Their pain, and stress their great shame
To the wider world.

Oyi[3]! *Jide ka ijii*[4].
Yes. Hold fast to what you have.
Today is theirs, the future yours.

---

[3] Dr. Okadigbo's traditional title.
[4] "*Jide ka ijii*" (Igbo) approximates to "hold fast to what you have", otherwise "keep it up".

THE RUBRIC

He called to me among the chanting crowds
Whose calls for good rule echoed from the clouds.
And now, in study, as the night descends,
My urge to brace his thoughtful words ascends.

I

Let's nod approval when acerbity
Shakes our state to foster probity.
Truth is piety, piety truth.
Their mission's half done who as one agree
To embrace truth from their youth.

Fools die and praise their fatherland in vain
Or extol a vain throne while they suffer pain.
And how improve our wizened posture then,
Like ghosts who fled the grave once and gain,
If we still stoop and dread our rulers' den?

Or douse our just wrath for some mortal boon,
While our dreaded ramparts fall and swoon?
Tortured by our leader's wand!
We'd rather die beneath an obscured moon
Than uphold unrighteous reprimand.

And may we perish doubly, here and there, beyond,
If we thwart one worthy praise, or opt to scorn
Or discount one deed of virtuous import,
Or sound one false note from one strident horn
To accord one baseless passion false support.

Patriotism is our taking care
To paint things as they are,
To not misname a spade,

And not shout of gloom, and flare,
When there's just a shade.

II

Like prudent herds, not given to delay,
Strive to find the dark goat while it's day,
Thus we must strive, and
Striving chase the thief of time away,
Lest the day should waste upon our hand.

Social sham must be dethroned and vanquished with
      satire.
Our oppressive elite must be cornered in full attire.
A wise land must have as its primal aim,
When all its walls are prone to blaze and ire,
To rout the vile cliques whence its troubles stem.

Who steals a crown should humbly bear the blame
If his rule defames his people's name.
They have a right to frown
At a king whose reign does not deserve acclaim,
And rise to seize their crown.

To he that's duly crowned the same applies,
If his tenure brings them only cries.
With their woes
He must be laden through; for, though he lives or dies,
He's one among their foes.

Since, viewed well on the other happy hand,
If a king, in ruling, strews a magic wand
That uplifts his people's name,
He will, until buried in their land,
Live to crave their acclaim.

III

Plato's thought remains the truest thing.
We rose to seek a philosopher king:
A mortal, yet a king divine.
We cry: farther depart more faithless trying
Than where strict oblivion may define!

And next to Plato stands our rare Rousseau:
Prompter of the quest in me – and you?
That timeless conscience of the world's misled!
Or yet, should leaders, while their role is true,
Not deign to take their footing from the led?

Our own true and chosen son will do,
If his ways are proven straight and true;
For no man is born to seek refuge
In his fatherland, or pester heaven before a prie dieu,
Being subject to a grinning stooge.

We want our son who knows our polity
Like the song thrush knows its melody.
For he'll rouse our wrath the more:
A new king whose throat is so unfree,
Spoilt, and fraught with foreign lore.

It's who steers a ship that wrecks its trip.
Where goes the shepherd there will go the sheep.
The while our sea borne nation goes adrift,
Who's at her helm, when not far asleep,
Is entangled in some trivial rift.

IV

They halve their worries that know what they want
And make it target of an earnest hunt.
We want a king, an upright ideologue.

Not the kind whose callowness must flaunt
As taught by many a mindless pedagogue.

And when arms shall have yielded to the gown[5],
If our throne's subjected to another clown,
To idly play and fumble with our crown,
Again, we shall rise with wrath and gusto, and march
    down,
To reclaim both the arm and the gown;

And impart more prudence to our waning throne,
And sting to wakefulness the drowsy drone.
These are the good plans of ill
Which, for another try, are yet forgone,
But which, in search of trust, we might fulfil.

And when we've shown misrule the way to ruin,
And proved ourselves the aimless clown's undoing,
Healed and one in clasp,
We shall know the end of all our ruing,
And ever keep our sceptre in our grasp.

Then, on earth, we shall attain to good,
And know the glory that is nationhood,
Whence the true Nigeria shall
Emerge: a nation, in her claim and attitude,
Worthy of the virtuous praise of all.

---

[5] The line, an adaptation of Cicero: "*Cedant arma togae*" (Let the arms yield to the gown) – De *Officiis* I.xxx.77.

ATHLETE

(To Dr. Edwin Madunagu[6])

You have kept the faith,
And yet are running the race
Against odds, breathing down
The twisted tracks,
A lone dragon.

Your tenacity inspires, energises us.
Yet we wait by the tracks,
Wary to join the race,
Applauding.

Marathoner, a blazing torch in hand,
Truth must feel a flash of pride,
Looking up from his lonely grave – at you!

---

[6] A Nigerian humanist and intellectual, possibly the country's last surviving Marxist ideologue.

GANI FAWEHINMI[7]

(Homage to a Noble Soul)

Of Gani, I too can tell some truth, tell
It straight and tell it nobly well.

The radiant soul, the dread of dark disdain,
The tough crown of our nation's virtuous men:

Strong and firm, insuperable, dyke
That guards the people and his like.

And gladly let me sing his noble ways,
Led on by disdain for fulsome praise.

Once a brave soul stood in Roman courts
and exuded thews of wit and lofty thoughts.

Cicero he was called and, true, he was
a man who spoke with a yet unrivalled force

until this great soul took birth in our land,
who tempers wit with truth on every hand.

Evil dreads him as darkness dreads the light
for good and only good brings him delight,

and valour, that when tempted to be vain
he'll pledge his dear life for the common man

or give his head, unruffled, to the noose,

---

[7] A Nigerian lawyer, politician and pro democracy activist.

that justice is not hanged without a fuss

as when a virtuous friend of his was killed,
by vermin, as the throne of falsehood willed?

He cares less though heavens fall
and stars miss their orbital spheres
and all the vainglorious quires squall
on earth without their bumptious airs.

For he cares to see our nation rise
above the fog of vice and gross misrule;
to see her rise before our very eyes,
above the sinking sand of ridicule.

THE HANDOUT

I quoted down the teacher word for word (at par
With Plato and with Theocritus),
But oh, the truth, my true and worthy sir
Marked me down for all his afflatus.

But when I took his handout[8] for a price (then
        brimmed
The better cup I sooner drank):
Now my honest work in school is trimmed,
My marks are worthy though my scripts are blank!

---

[8] Handout: the generic name for mimeographed lecture notes widely sold by lecturers in Nigerian tertiary institutions.

TO FIDEL...

I have arisen and walked through the shadows.
There is no justice even here.
I shall march with you to the gallows.
And let the noose be near!

New monstrous worms of vice and decadence
are eating up our university.
And the votaries of truth and conscience
are staple fare for their voracity.

The wings of liberal thought are clipped
with us. A teacher wants me in
for "The Handout"[9]. And someone has quipped,
"Does wit equal capital sin?"

You too must hang for you will
not deny an obvious spade.
Some little tyrants hungry for a kill
have yielded all for lurking in the shade.

Courage, friend! Not to worry.
You are not alone, good dear.
I, too, am neither cursed, nor sorry,
that I'm other than the breed that fear.

---

[9] The preceding poem.

A YEAR AFTER

(To "Piper")

you were whisked away that fine morning...
with your father... it was said...
the rest is a tale of woe and mourning
spawning aches and puzzles in my head...

they snatched you from home... the Bakassi[10]...
that keep our troubled peace the savage way...
and from that grim odyssey
your father returned... but you were *put away*...

the weals that marred his body said it all...
how *confessions* were dragged from son and father...
and... as cruelly as the tales recall...
each was tortured to forswear the other...

now the silence of a father who watched his
son slaughtered cannot be broken... and I
reflect and ask what went amiss...
for while you died the law was standing by...

but time sits upon his throne and will judge...
their grief has not been brief that loved you...
and still love you... though the streets misjudge
and call you villain... adieu Piper... adieu!

---

[10] The Bakassi, a dreaded vigilante group, operates in some states of South eastern Nigeria.

DAWN OF DEMOCIDE[11]

(To Obi Nwakanma[12])

We woke up that morning to see that the hawks
Had swooped down on our brood.
Our death imbrued nest rose up in squawks
As they tore their quarries on their iron rood.
We sought the courage to express our pains
And you gave it to us –
No shenanigans!

Truth and justice are chicks in the talons of hawks.
And won't they eat him on their rood
If Christ returned sans glory who ignored the squawks
Of our plundered, guiltless brood?
And if he sought to scream out his pains
Would you lend him a voice?
No shenanigans!

It's still a nation where the monk's the cowl,
A nation with a golden begging bowl;
Of little fragile innocents torn apart
And pierced to the heart
By the talons of their predators.
Yet let the palm go to our violators
Whilst you boldly ventilate our pains.
No shenanigans!

To leave our conscience hedged with cowardice

---

[11] A coinage, *democide* can be translated as *killing of the people* and be considered to have occurred each time a government or any of its agencies is culpable for the unlawful death of a citizen.
[12] A Nigerian poet and scholar.

Is, at length, to hasten our demise.
Our saucers gleam with thistles and with lies.
From a shattered roost a hen cries
To the bird that sings tongue in cheek
And to the other bird of double speak.
And if like her I sought to vent my spleen
Would you lend me a voice?
No shenanigans!

Okigwe[13] was a feast for democide!
And yet the hunters belch, caress their maws,
Preen themselves and sidle side to side.
From the gathering clouds a raven caws:
No shenanigans!

---

[13] In an early morning raid in February 2001 the Nigerian Police reportedly shot about ten suspected members of the Movement for the Actualisation of the Sovereign State of Biafra (MASSOB) at Okigwe, a town in south eastern Nigeria, and inflicted serious injuries on several others.

THE SCAPEGOAT

All hail the ghost of our invocations!
Exeunt vérité et sens commun! Entre équivocations!

You were there
For two score years
Or more,
And left
A body hollow
At its core.

Now a man
Does not fill the hole while he can
And strings your names
To tie his sheaf of blames.

Yours the guilt
The day his milk turned sour,
And his watch
Skipped an hour,
The rump that pumps
His rumbling flatulence.

Last night the Ghost of Four
Reared up in my sleep.
Their bodies dripped with gore.
And their pallor faked the frozen deep.
Said one: "They ruined our souls
Who guard a man that judged
His life at risk. And their weapon
Was the soldiers' too!"
"And your name?" I asked.
"Onyebuchi Ede."

How long you've been gone!
Three years now by May!
Yet our beans turn to stones.
And our nights encroach upon our days.
And our magic hand
Holds up his wand,
Enacts exorcisms, that you may be gone!

And should he
Accuse you
Ten years hence – yes, ten years hence –
Would you wish your kind were never there?

THESE I HAVE LOVED

EMISSARY

I hold a pigeon in my hands,
Bred for home and alien lands,
I hope the pigeon understands
Why it's in my hands.

I yearn to fly to everyone
With a heart that's free from strife and stone
And tell them in a gentle tone
That every soul is one.

TO A SPARROW

And you came to harm for livelihood:
entrapped by man's ungainly attitude
till his snare severed your gentle leg
and left your body dangling by a peg.

How true that the hurtful thread is gone!
While its graver harm is yet undone?
Rather stay with me and have a cure.
Those in need of healing must endure.

I shan't let you go now that your pain
does not let you rise above the plain
where it lurks with venom, like the shrew,
the adder whose fangs know no pity too.

Yes. Freedom is the right of all that live.
The union is folly that makes us grieve.
But be sure to go the day it's healed:
this wound that a bleeding gash revealed.

THE CHICKS

> (Lines set to an encounter with a friend before I
> retrieved the birds from a trench one stormy
> evening)

Yes, I hear "the rumbling sky's alarm".
And "how the hastening clock of evening ticks!"
But look, some fellow travellers come to harm.
See, the lily white unhappy chicks.

I too must heed the anguish of their souls,
And keep my vow to nature once again.
And here, again, the deafening thunder growls:
"The heavens come to dip the earth in rain!"

But hark, they whimper from within a trench:
"Where fate entrapped our luckless souls since noon."
And smell the evil of their prison's stench.
See, the horror of the spying moon.

You may hasten home and have your rest,
For faster faster still the timer ticks!
But how their cries of anguish pierce my breast,
That I must jump within and raise the chicks.

EUTHANASIA

Your last day, yes, is coming,
weary *Agama* lizard,
in a season you're moulting,
tree climbing wizard.

You drag your body like a slug
distraught with pain and grief.
You're more confused, yes, than a log
trapped in the yellow leaf[14].

I came with hopes to hear you scream,
and start with fright, and flee.
But you stayed, unmoved, as in a dream,
and blinked your eyes on me.

I stamped my feet upon the ground.
Then you woke from your trance.
And with pride, suicidal, pranced around
in death's macabre dance.

I'm not inclined to take your life,
though you wish to die.
Life as man is full of strife.
I, too, wished it passed me by.

---

[14] The line, an adaptation of line 5 of Lord Byron's poem: "On This Day I Complete My Thirty sixth Year".

APOLOGIA

(On reading Tanure Ojaide's[15] "The Fate of Vultures")

The murderous eagle earns a worthy name.
The vulture eats the dead and dies in blame.

Good old patient vulture waiting:
Still waiting to feed from the hand of death.
The smirching of your name is not abating.
And none will sing your praise upon the earth.

The bloody eagle tears his murdered prey.
And he's a "noble" bird.
And you – whose ration comes from death's decay –
Are "infamous" and "weird".

"He's deemed the better who must hunt to eat,"
You brood and wonder why,
"With talons dripping with another's meat:
Earth's monarch of the sky."

"They call him worthy for his show of strength,
If strength is kill the weak,"
But will not reckon with your endless length
Of patience none can break.

How our minds oppress with prejudice!
How shallow when we judge!
And that you long to live with less of this:
Our unwarranted grudge!

---

[15] A Nigerian poet and scholar.

To A Murdered Egret

What must have killed you, oh egret,
and trampled on your corpse without regret?
What must have stilled your sinless wings?
Tell me, what, of all lower mortal things?

What loveless soul which beauty makes more sick
could deign to work with such a bloodied stick
that struck you squarely – lying in a bog
to await the vulture or the scrounging dog?

Your killer must have thought himself a man,
whose wisdom smiled on such a foolish plan.
O pity! Soar to heaven with your soul.
Let me do the grieving as a whole

and tell your killer how he's less than brute.
For though a wolf were lost in wanton youth,
would it fall as such to turpitude,
in search of fun, and not for want of food?

TO AN INJURED RAT

Poor drenched rat limping in the rain,
What a trauma you are wading through!
Did you abscond from a ratter's zoo
Who in frantic pursuit caused you pain
Or escape a rattrap or a ditch
Concealed by a hunter or a witch?

Your right hind limb – I sure can see –
Is sprained and needs a special cure.
Come, I pledge to pay the doctor's fee.
He will ease your painful state – for sure!

Come, suffering rat, I urge you – come!
Why still limp – and limp away from me?

THE QUESTION

I

In the Nigerian Conservation Foundation[16]
We are in the vanguard of earth's preservation.
We have no homes in the sky.
So we shall not let her die.

And you, who shun the call to protect her,
Who foul the rivers and pollute the seas,
Who let out poisonous fumes upon the air,
And tear up timeless forests by their roots, ah!
You, if she's killed at last,
Just what will be your fate?

II

The countless precious trees we've logged to death,
The "lower" lives we plunder through the earth,
The birds of flight we call it sport to shoot,
That gasp beneath our thickening cloud of soot,
And oh, those victims of our poaching greed;
If earth, our anguished mother, dies at last,
Just what will be your fate?

III

The just and proper sense of being man
Is not to ruin the world the worst we can.
The claim we lay to superiority
May yet be proved with sensitivity.
Or can't our human heart be better used
To love the earth, our earth, with tenderness?

---

[16] The poet is an affiliate of the Nigerian Conservation Foundation (NCF).

But all you who will bring her life to ruin
And not know that you work your own undoing,
If she dies at last,
Just what will be your fate?

PANDRILLUS[17]

(For Paddy, Liza, Peter)

Paddy[18], come. Come and see what Liza and Peter have done!

Come. Don't wait at the gate. Come and see how they have civilized an antelope. But you must put down your hunting gun.

Tunde: the antelope's name! A Sitatunga! He's a model of geniality. He will meet you at the door of his pen, nozzle at your outstretched hand, lick it in greeting, and wait! And that's just morning for his pleasantries.

If you stayed he would dig at the pen floor with his stout horns, strike a combat pose, and feign to lock horns with an absent foe.

Then be sure to rub his proffered flanks and congratulate our maestro of the solitary ring bout, our modern Don Quixote!

Thrice I watched his antics to the end and chose to call him Don... Don for short.

Liza says "he's so tame he'll follow a hunter home"[19]. Then between him and the hunter who will be the beast? I'm keen to have your answer once you're in. But why

---

[17] Pandrillus is the project name of a drill rehabilitation and breeding centre in Calabar, established by the American conservationists: Liza Gadsby and Peter Jenkins.

[18] Paddy Ezeala, an environmental activist, is the Communications Manager of the Nigerian Conservation Foundation (NCF).

[19] Less than a year after this jovial remark Tunde was killed by a hunter following his transfer to a forest reserve in Lagos.

still make delays? Just lay your rifle down!

Is that your hunting dog I hear his bark? Leave him at the gate!

In the West the sun descends and soaks its downward path in amber light!

And Aniefiok, chieftain of the drill clan, struts his cage domain. There's a conscious swagger in his gait: a locomotory thumping of the chest. A macho drill! Lords it over the rest! But who was worthier with a two inch tooth, and a rainbow mane across his chest?

There he goes, oh so leisurely, rocking at the waist and shoulder joints. A turn with a swivel! A glance over the shoulder! A thumb to the nose! He pads the floor, silently.

There he goes again, a prankish string of offspring at his tail. "Only those from his loins." The keeper says. They are at the drinking trough. His "harem" scatters save "his favourite". The keeper…

They lap up water, with the children in their father's wings.

He glares at what? O, it's you coming!

Now that's how he departs. A monkey's majesty! Grunting. Making faces. Flashing his canines. Heading for his palace. Grunting.

CHILD OF MAN

Despised and unheeded, you stand in the rain
And think that life is meant for cold and pain.
So it is!
For thought has gone amiss,
And pity slain
Upon the stony shrine of cruel disdain.

You must brace to bear your rood alone,
Though your brittle shoulders break unblown.
Cease to mope
At fast receding hope.
Nor stay forlorn,
Grieving at the gloating sneers of scorn.

Ever will you be the child of man,
And victim of his earth's distorted plan.
Ever will you
Know your friends are few
In joy; and in pain,
Learn to bear the heartless shrugs of men.

WEEP NOT, CHILD

Weep not, child.
Though your hope has died,
and not a soul is standing by your side.

Weep not for a world that's full of gore,
where the rich must live upon the poor
and the high leave the low to "die, or endure".

Weep not for the charms
of a world that starves its farms
and feeds its populace with deadly arms.

Stay your fears,
wet no patch of earth with needless tears
as angels bear the pain to sing your cares.

All these shall come to pass.
The gross, the vain, the foolish and the crass
shall someday come to nothing in the mass.

More fairylands of bliss are soon to come,
where every starving child could live in a dome
and lonesome toddlers make the trees their home.

But if I may ask and stroke your head,
and lay across your palms a loaf of bread,
then, Black Child, will you be alive or dead?

SHEAVES OF PASSION

UYI MY BOYHOOD'S LAST LOVE

I had set my thoughts against celestial airs
To grasp angels' forms ascending heaven's stairs.
But now, with me, known beauty most divine
Endures and blooms as mine – Uyi is mine!

No virtue thought to dwell in heaven's gate
Shall lure me but the beauty of this mate
Whom my dreams are spread upon her way
That she may tread on them from day to day.

Illusion. Passion. Pack your wares and flee!
I've found a thing to hold eternally:
A perfect soul, a woman made complete;
A love, a joy, a future fair to breathe.

Eternal seems her freshness like the wind
That makes woods and meadows blow so kind.
And thus, by heaven, she is sent to bless
My soul with goodness dearer than happiness.

LYRIC FOR UYI (I)

How so brightly Uyi smiles,
How so sunnily,
That, farther from a million miles,
She's known with certainty.

How her hips, in rhythm, move
With cute steps one by one!
She'll make any man sick with love,
Be he flesh or stone.

How so courtly in her speech,
How confident too,
How in pride and beauty rich,
How in manner pure!

Call her earth's most pure delight,
A bright angelic light,
A beauty full in heaven's sight,
You'll in all be right.

LYRIC FOR UYI (II)

(Of all the things that cheer and bless)

Of all the things that cheer and bless,
My love is, true, the norm:
A perfect piece of loveliness
That wears a human form.

She has a heart that's true and rare,
With such a burning zone!
And ivory teeth, and dusky hair,
That'll make an angel moan.

She's such a jewel, precious pearl,
Upon a silver hill,
A lake of gold, an endless thrill,
To cherish, and to feel.

O, how I'm greater than a king!
And should I dare be less?
With a goddess, as a human being,
To worship, and possess.

LUCKY ROSE

Go, lucky rose.
Go now to the one I love.
Go with sunshine streaming from above,
and wet her nose.

Go and wet her nose with morning dew.
Go as sweet and red.
Light the cheerless pallor of her bed,
with flames of you.

Go, for dawn is cheering from above.
And the bird of early spring
joins to sing:
"Lucky is the rose that wakes my love!"

SERENADE

> (For singing, preferably, and with instrumental accompaniment)

Ever, was she such a joy to see:
Fairer than the morning sun in June?
And what can so delight the soul of me
Like the rustle of her infant tune?

True, by virtue, she is tall and trim:
Taller, trimmer, than a joy can be;
A vase of beauty stainless to the brim,
Shaped for bliss and immortality!

And though it's not for muffled love I sing,
I fain would love her reckless beauty still,
Like a weak and truly mortal thing:
Quick to lose his bearings and his will.

Who will hold her in a tame surprise
That's scaled the wall that hid her charms from me,
That's stood to wonder at her dreamy eyes:
Like a mermaid drifting on the sea?

OMEN

So long I endured the crickets shrill,
their stridulating in the evening chill,
and the cat whose ceaseless caterwaul
proclaimed her rutting season to a wall.

Then I asked the one I called my mate:
Is it life that yields such fruits of hate
to a creature who forfeits his heart for love
or who, for nothing, sinks his soul in art?

So long she regarded me with spite,
through the leaden shadows of the night:
so hard of hearing is her inner ear
to hear the cat and crickets that I hear.

A NUPTIAL FLIGHT

The shade is sombre in an aged tree
Where we sit and watch them ply the sky.
The pair of toucan shuttles by in glee!
How they clap their joyous wings on high
And seem to fly from love's impending sigh!

And here sit I – with whom I now love,
Or think I love – and watch them chart
Their nuptial flight above. How they rove
The blue and mistless sky, each trusting heart
Glad as if their ways will never part.

Thus flew I at the dawn of my old lost love,
With wings out stretched, as if immune to scorn.
The one I loved and I, then as these above,
We steered our flight towards the rising sun,
And cruised as if his race would not be run.

But now I sit in this tree's sombre shade
Grieving in another's arms her loss,
In her arms that prop the head
That lolls upon my breast, to think remorse
Will part the pair like us!

THE RECEPTIONIST

Gladdened heart entrusted to a card,
Though the route be weary, long and hard,
Go, tell the one you've loved to hear her moan
How sweet she sounds across the telephone.

And like a homer, steadfast in your flight,
Bring back tidings of her own delight.
But be sure to yield the hope to her,
That lifts the moon beside a shining star.

DEPARTURE

The moon is burning with a fading light.
The stars are altogether out of sight.
My heart is sullen and my face is grey,
For morning comes to take my love away:

A woman graceful like a full gazelle,
Her smile, a gladdener, like a drink of ale.
But morning comes to take her out of sight,
And stop the fountain of my new delight.

But love and loved one let me dare to pray
That peace and all the graces lead your way.
But don't go gladly, nor stay long apart,
For you are going away with my heart.

GIRL IN MY CLASS

There's a girl in my class:
A sweet and lovely lass
With glassy eyes
And teeth as white as ice.

She's tall, svelte, brunette,
And more than all the wonder of our set.

Her gait is debonair,
And it's wavy with her silky hair,
And all our eyes love her, and commend her:
That earthly beauty brighter than a star!

And yes my heart once went to her
And never returned,
And never shall return,
For I never wanted it back!

THE DANCE

I came off with memories of the dance.
And my heart is poor
in words to tell its joy for the chance
to have seen you command the floor;

to have danced with you, and danced:
the pupil of your solemn expertise;
your hips in my hands,
my eyes to your eyes;

and to have found, young girl,
reasons – reasons yet as never before –
why my heart, as now, must whirl
in flight to you to ask for more.

SONG: TO IJ

Truly is a rose a work of art
that gladdens nature and the human heart.
Truly is a rose a thing of joy:
the floral answer to the Dame of Troy.

But why, dear bud and flower of my joy,
true to beauty like the Dame of Troy,
have you bred a canker in my heart
and saddened nature as a work of art?

CALL HER BELINDA

>(For singing, preferably, with chorus and light music)

The plump and glorious flower stands apart,
Like the perfect mystery of the heart.
If you love the splendour of the art,
Sing her praise and call her Belinda!

The reckless beauty in her form expressed;
The passion in her glances unsuppressed;
If your soul is true and unrepressed,
Sing her praise and call her Belinda!

She's like morning when the night was long,
And her rays are gentle more than strong,
Like a star her days on high are young,
Sing her praise and call her Belinda!

Her lips rosy, like a fountain, glad,
Sweet in smile and spouting joy like mad;
And though you lack the madness I have had,
Sing her praise and call her Belinda!

The strands of fire you will call her hair;
The sweet and quiet of her radiant air;
If your love of what is good is fair,
Sing her praise and call her Belinda!

What known beauty of the perfect form
Could mean pleasure like her stress and storm?
This heart disquiet you may think the norm,
Sing her praise and call her Belinda!

From the perfect form of what is seen
Know the form of what is yet unseen;
And though your eyes as well as mine are green,
Sing her praise and call her Belinda!

LOVE

I wake today with a simple aim:
to write you a simple poem
and say that I care, truly,
that I have loved your charm and modesty.

But such words desert me as I crave,
hard as I have
tried to have them
incorporated in my poem, your poem.

When, in that same room yesterday,
as we conversed, and our eyes met
in one quick, benignant glance,
and your lips stretched
in that supple smile whose depth
I could not fathom,
and your face coloured with a blush
as you averted your eyes
more mysteriously from mine,
I longed to take your hand
and say that I'm sure,
that I'll be good to you,
but there were other people all about!

O that it would be lost on you
how sweet you looked,
unless you faced the mirror
in my eyes!
But your impulse was
to look away,
till the waiting mirror
froze your doubts.

A NEW DEAL

O that you could know how your hesitation
affects the faith I profess, and that
you could come with me on this one journey
and the rest of the journeys
I shall make on life's ringed road.

This much I know, that a woman
like you – so beautiful, so companionable, and yet so
sensible – must have loved.
And that you could leave
those clutters from your past
and follow me into a new deal,
and I shall lead you on to fix the fragments
of your broken faith, your faith in love and life.

The task will be tough, the journey rough, I agree.
But I shall try my best.

Quite often to have failed
is simply not to have dared.

Then for what in return do I hope? To share
that strength and resilience you are, and in so doing
wind up stabilized, that I may become
anchored in time's tempestuous sea.
O resolute plant, tough tendrils, climbing skywards
from such lowly soil, that I may learn to climb
and climb with you. Yes, I think I'm true.
But your faith will make me truer still.

The hour is early yet.
Outdoors the crickets still sing.

And I have longed for your presence
at the height of this meditation,
that I may, fallen to my knees,
touch my cooling forehead at your feet.

DIRGE

Did I say it would come to this?
No fraud escapes the searching hands of light.
And falsehoods, sown, germinate in shame.

Angel of our smudged transparencies,
At love's checkerboard of delight
Those who play victim botch the game.

They botch the game and turn delight amiss
By their carping calls to their victim plight
And their sleight of hand shuffles of blame.

Thus, between you and I, the door of bliss
Was nailed shut by the hand of the night
That swore faith and cheated all the same.

And yet my final word amounts to this:
I reared thoughts to turn my wrongs to right
And do not charge the blame against your name.

OMNIBUS

ON THE PULSE OF THE MILLENNIUM

Today, tonight, this moment,
You can judge yourself a name in heavenly light;
Like a Castor, a Pollux,
A Perseus, or an Andromeda, perhaps.

For just take another leap – no, a stride
Will do – and you have made history!
Or, if you can do none of these,
Just wait, wait for the clock
To tick once more – just once more – and you
Are there with the fortunate and the strong!

Now think of the meaning, the great grand
        significance:
Never, never again shall
Such day, such night, such moment
Engulf the whole world
For another thousand years!

O to have been there,
To have shared the tension
And the thrill, a dancing mote
In the beam of the universe!

Now the sky is decked with stellar light,
The moon, resplendent, sails before our sight,
The foliage of our planet – if you see –
Plume themselves and sway with greenery,
Your heart can reach for a joy it never knew before,
And never shall know again. No, nevermore!

And yet a joy that, for all its brevity,
Many might have wished they joined to share:
Standing on this brief eternity,
The dawning moment of a thousandth year.

And all you who can share the first pulse
Of a millennium fresh in its cradle,
Fortunate heirs to the treasure
That is today, tonight, this moment,
Arise!
Take your neighbour's hand
And say – ever so gratefully –
Welcome to the dawn of a new era,
Come and live and be at rest[20].

And sing:

> An old long era has passed by,
> And in has come a new:
> So great the event that earth and sky
> Rejoice with me, and you!
>
> O mark it with a brilliant show!
> A cheerful noise unheard:
> Two greatest ages men can know
> Enact a change of guard.

---

[20] The line alludes to the meaning traditionally ascribed to Calabar, where the poem was first read in public.

THE CHALLENGER

> (On the first remembrance of the crash of the space shuttle Challenger)

The Challenger.
What a prophetic name!
Like America had known
That you'd be more than just a space shuttle,
But one with a great challenge
To her and all mankind.

The space shuttle Challenger!
You cheerfully went up the sky
Propelled by thunderous ovations below.
But soon struck by the hand of fate,
You came down, down with the stuff you had:
A challenge to America and all mankind.

O Challenger!
We hope you'll rise again in triumph.

INDICTMENTS

His sea is misted for tomorrow.
His heart suckles on the breast of sorrow.
The holed in rats of splendour stare at him,
Vacantly.

His axe in blossom long before his limbs,
His scythe is sharp until the reaping starts,
From the teats of night his lips are torn,
Forcefully.

His mind is reeling in animism.
He chews the flower of his canticles,
Fortnightly.

The proud messiah with a broken heart
Leaves a rood and resurrects in art,
Frequently.

And the timeless sea of indifference
Girds the world and drowns the martyr still,
Dismally.

And the prickly petals of his rose
Exude their tigrish charm of violence,
Constantly.

At length the lightening in his infant eyes
Clashes with the thunder in his voice,
Radially.

REMINISCENCE

(Of a Church Bazaar witnessed in Childhood)

It is written, "My house shall be called a house of prayer…"

— Matthew 21:13 (RSV)

Three men, in pious gambling, shared a dice
by one kiosk where I checked a grocer's price.
They fouled the sweet air with the stench of greed,
like beings whose doings professed God – indeed!

While there, one fellow sought to read my palms,
where despised beggars strained and pined for alms,
who came, I sensed, to get help from the Lord,
through men who proudly claimed to live His Word.

From far, the auctioneer's shrill voice came aloud,
like thunder, shrieking, charges through the cloud.
The biddings soared, the trained announcer grinned,
as each bidder, toppled, felt chagrined.

I stood and watched their hell bound business train.
I was yet a lad. My mind was young.
Yet I knew the time was ripe again:
to bring His horsewhip to the synagogue.

JOLLY SIDE EXCHANGE

As the tavern bubbled yesterday,
A drunk was singing to his smoking friend:

"I declare smoking adiaphorous but sometimes think I
      lie.
For it seems to me that smokers, when they die,
Are massed on high and then flushed back to earth
To live until they've cleansed their stinking breath."

And then the smoker to the drunken man,
Coughing out the white fumes as he sang:

"But back on earth some give their lives to drinking,
And go carousing till they lose their thinking.
Thus they change their old ways in the main,
But never get to make it up again."

LITTLE WOMEN; LITTLE GIRLS

(Lyric occasioned by listening to a conversation
on Dr. Eka Williams's daughters)

Little women; little girls:
fairer than the dawn!
Could you lift your gaze awhile
and look across the lawn?

You cast a shadow of a light
that's thickly dense in gold,
that all will see and then be right
to reckon – and behold.

They say your shadow and your hue
are like your mother's – true! –
and make gold of the morning dew
upon the grasses – too.

They say your shadow of her light –
along the passes – shine –
that marvel at her human sight
of human light divine.

But then they wonder if your days –
if one and one is two –
will pass from beauty into good,
like that your mother's – too.

THOUGHTS BY SKY AND SEA

(To Dr. Kalu Ojah)

At each season I send my noblest thoughts to you;
Through the winds
That skim the clouds
And bridge eternities;
At each season I send my noblest thoughts to you,
Pure thoughts of peace profound.

At each season I send my noblest thoughts to you;
Across the seas,
Across the waves,
Across the seething foam;
My noblest thoughts, though ruffled by the storms,
Shall find their ways to you.

TOURNAMENT IN JEBBA

(For Hamzat Ibrahim[21], Knight of FIDE)

A king is losing ground
Against a pawn, a rook,
And warlike knights.
The all forbidden comes!
The truth of winning
At the game of chess:
A pride is floored.
An empire falls.
It is checkmate!

But I – poet of the world
And the wandering heart –
Must fete this rural city
Massed with rocks,
Where I have seen
My first baobab
Stout by the Niger
That rolls its endless water
Through our dams.

Hamzat, your good has brought us here.
Shepherd more than worthy of his flock,
May our joy in your days be long,
And last forever true.

The end is near at last,
As glory clamours in embrace of loss,
And I – poet of the world
And the wandering heart –
Arise and take my leave.

---

[21] A former Managing Director of the National Electric Power Authority (NEPA).

MUTUAL PROPS

Two trees that might have fallen
Are leaning on each other.
Slanted are their
Half uprooted trunks,
On whose heads
A crown of flowers
Blooms, and draws
May heart's affection
To its charm.

O worthy sign
Of how compassion works,
That I may lend
A falling friend
A hand, and find
At long last
That I helped myself!

A Stellar Monologue

O lone star!
That decks
The heavens
Like a lustrous gem:
Bright, hot, pulsating
In a dark, lone, deserted sky.

Amid a host of stars
You will still be.
But, then, how distinguished?

Thus it happens
With our lives below,
That we may need
Aloneness in the dark
To stress the vigour
Of the light
We bear.

INTERROGATION

The *Mona Lisa* hanging on my wall,
loved and much adored by one and all.
What is your content but beauty?
Say, what else is your moral duty?
Are you not a proof that, all alone,
Beauty too can stand and hold its own?

As what is largely moral, yes, can stand,
like that *Guernica* from Picasso's hand.

And though it's better thought that pulchritude
in art should strike a moral attitude,
you prove that charm – sheer charm – can satisfy,
that beauty – all alone – can edify.

A CLOWN'S TOAST

I've fixed a latch upon my heart
And stopped its search for good.
If you're not my lost rib,
Then I didn't lose a rib.

Nor will I yet be keen to find
The rib I seemed to lose,
Knowing – if its loss were true –
You weren't made from it.

A Lunatic in the Library

Chequered, brusque and crusty
are his looks,
as he mutters sayings
which no reader brooks
and dog ears a musty book
from page to page
and sneers and snickers
at a printed sage,
and then a curious grin
adorns his face,
this madman who is so in love with books.

Beside my seat
he studied yesterday,
and he's seated
next to me today.
He murmurs yet again
and wrings his hands,
and feigns to lodge thoughts
in his cranial files.
Again the curious grin
upon his face,
this madman who is so in love with books.

Perhaps, tomorrow,
he'll be here again;
perhaps the next day
and the next day still.
Perhaps he'll come
to make me wonder more:
what lies behind
his plight, and what before,

that *L o o n y*, as engraved
upon his looks,
he still seeks treasure daily in the books.

CRADLE SONG

(For Roseanne Orim)

"Welcome. Welcome."
I hear an angel by your cradle side.
"The gates of life and joy are open wide,
Welcome!"

"Welcome. Welcome."
I hear the chaste and glorious choir sing.
"Endless is the joy a birth can bring,
Welcome!"

"Welcome. Welcome."
An early bird is singing in the dew.
And all the hosts of heaven say to you,
"Welcome!"

I HEARD YOU WERE STABBED

(To Naguib Mafouz)

I heard[22] you were stabbed! Stabbed! – that
the daggers nearly pierced your heart –
as the hounds at morning had their day,
and hate, usurping virtue, had its way.

I heard you were sprawling on the ground,
ripped at neck and breast by hound and hound;
that, truly, it was morning turned to night,
as darkness, baneful, sought the throne of light.

But, whatever heard, you know better than I:
your kindred souls are set above the sky,
above the common ground of hounds and earth
where men fight reason with the tools of death.

---

[22] The BBC broadcast the attack on the Egyptian 1988 Nobel laureate in literature in October 1994.

FREE AMONG THESE HILLS

When shall banners rise among these hills?
Banners of our longing to be free!
O maternal city,
When shall they?

Far from home we're still a horde disdained.
The wrongs they charge to us are not explained.
We're scorned by hosts we fawn like dogs to please,
And hated worse than fleas.

When shall banners rise among these hills?
Banners of our right to dignity!
O maternal city,
When shall they?

And yet our lions root for scraps of meat,
(A sea has rolled its sleeves to drown its shore)
Suckled long by vixens with deceit,
They thrive on nothing more.

They slit their veins to fight an alien's cause,
Trail a bloated paunch,
Lacerate our hunch.

Shall they ever rise among these hills?
Banners of our yearning to be free!
Free from lack and worry, O be free,
Free among these hills!

SPIRIT OF THE AGE?[23]

Why would they jump off a gilt tower,
Dropping down the sky
Like rags of fear?

Peace is on the scaffold.
And hate gloats over her
Headless body with a bloodied axe.

Dropping down the sky,
Blasted off the mountaintop
Of sense, shredded up, falling,
Scattering in their tatters
As they fell.

Peace is on the scaffold.
And hate gloats over her
Headless body with a bloodied axe.

And we heard the bangs
That shook our world,
The clenched fisted bangs
Of hate, of dry, stone hard hate
Bringing down the doors
Of our collective faith.
O that we could
Only stare helpless,
Fixed to the earth with rivets
Of horror, numbed, motionless!

---

[23] Composed in response to "Like a Typical American Movie", an article by Olusegun Adeniyi, a Nigerian journalist, on the September 11 terrorist attack on the World Trade Centre, published on the back page of *THISDAY* of September 20, 2001.

Peace is on the scaffold.
And hate gloats over her
Headless body with a bloodied axe.

Yet must we cry blood?
Where was blood the fluid
To wash off blood?

But if we give them water
Will they drink?

If we take the mantle
Of peace to them
Will they accept,
And not reduce
The love we bear
To shreds?

NOCTURNE

Tonight!
Abuja is a city in light,
A glittering dark shawl flaunting its delight
To the pleasure of sight.

The roads have kept their endless streams
Of light – crystal beams
Of amber, neon and white –
Meandering through the mystic night.

The motorcades sustain their leisured flow
In a city mysteriously aglow,
Tranquil, still,
As I stand on the Strabag Hill.

TROPICAL FACTS

The mighty ship
will get nowhere
except on the back
of a river.

The Iroko,
monarch of the trees,
that wears the crown
of the forest;
yes, that mightiest
and hardiest
of our trees
was once
a sapling.

The lion
roars the jungle
into fright.
But, if you know,
he was once
a helpless,
fragile cub.

And that envy
of the avian world:
the eagle
making spirals
in its flight,
soaring in
a bright
azure sky,
was a fledgling once.

Even the king,
if he's haughty,
was a child
that pissed
in its cradle!

And all the expert jesters
in his court,
that make him
quake and crackle
at the ribs,
were they
upstarts once?

THE PASSAGE

(To Dr. Pius Okigbo[24])

The wind had quenched our flame amid the night
Our heart was heavy that our guess was right
We lifted up our eyes and what a sight!

>As you passed the comets filled the sky
>But were far too shocked with grief to fly.

And soon we'd reckon that we knew you not
That our bond had lacked a mystic knot
But such were ironies we soon forgot

>As you passed the comets filled the sky
>But were far too shocked with grief to fly.

Need we know a life to feel its worth?
As they know the king that hail him forth?
Their facial temblor wrinkles at the North

>As you passed the comets filled the sky
>But were far too shocked with grief to fly.

Be proud to heed the loud ancestral call
Weighted with festoons and standing tall
Lights, most bright, are memories after all

>As you passed the comets filled the sky
>But were far too shocked with grief to fly.

---

[24] A Nigerian economist and brother to the poet, Christopher Okigbo (referred to as Chris in the poem) killed in 1969 by federal troops during the Nigerian Civil War.

And when beyond you meet the likes of Chris
Tell them that as yet we face the blitz
That our common scourge has come to this

> As you passed the comets filled the sky
> But were far too shocked with grief to fly.

Tell them how our fates are still gang chained
To those same ills for which their blood was drained
That the spite we suffered has remained

> As you passed the comets filled the sky
> But were far too shocked with grief to fly.

Tell them we are proud they spent for us
The lives they earned too nobly for remorse
But then we've ever lived to mourn our loss

> As you passed the comets filled the sky
> But were far too shocked with grief to fly.

We pledge no will a battering ram can break
In vain they labour to profane our ache
Our yoke shall sprout with lilies for their sake

> As you passed the comets filled the sky
> But were far too shocked with grief to fly.

Tell Chris that our garlands wait for him
That yet we draw our waters from his stream
And drink his honeyed words and live his dream

> As you passed the comets filled the sky
> But were far too shocked with grief to fly.

Our drums are silent and our gongs are numb
Their tearful hollowed throats are strangely dumb
They strain with occult gestures to be mum

> As you passed the comets filled the sky
> But were far too shocked with grief to fly.

METAPHORS

A pine dips her neck and sighs,
Sighs to the wind.
The hooting of a distant owl derides
The sorrows in her mind.

On my wall a rendezvous begins,
Of cats and dogs and mice.
And a tinny tribe of manikins
Floats before my eyes.

It's with gloating that some fears arrive
To detonate our dreams.
And they roam abroad as lesser lives,
And elves that dance on streams.

IT WAS HIS DOUBTS

It was his doubts. It was – yes – his doubts.
Could he muster hate in such a guise?
Could he rip your back with iron prongs?
Or hide in scowling eyes?

And the razor of envenomed tongues
May draw our blood the while the battle lasts,
And furious nails invade our supple flesh,
And wind words strike us with their chilling blasts.

But patiently, patiently, press
On to the prize:
The tender tigress
In a fierce disguise.

AFTER CHRYSALIS

On a citrus tree a butterfly is waiting.

Wings of radiance and naivety,
Waiting to fly.

Waiting beside a shell puparium,
It worms its thoughts to darkness and to doubt.

And it waits.
After chrysalis, the butterfly waits.

Waits on delicate half deserted wings
Splashed with colour like the peacock's back.

O that it might bawl
At the threshold, given voice.

So it must wait — pensively, in calm, sedately —
To clothe its puzzled mind
In seedy time.

And wait it does, dazzled
By a sham kaleidoscope.

And lunch its flight it must.
Or wait, half impaled
On a cross of angst.

O it glides off at last!
Gains height.
Bumps across the distance
As it flies:

Is it a world where dreams die unlamented?
Where no nectar gluts the palms
Of generous blooms?
Where we must forage for sweetness,
If sweetness can be found
Within its bounds?

O patient puzzler of the dusty wings,
Fly!

APPENDIX
(For children, especially)

The Preacher and the Voice

I

Arise and go to Nineveh!
There are souls to deliver.
It's the master lodged in you.
So don't question why.

II

And I lived and preached abroad.
And none would turn from sin
Or care a whit to hear the word
Of he that's lodged in me.
And just back from those distant lands
He must revive my shame
And goad as if he understands
That zeal can lose its flame.

III

Hey! Don't grumble my dear man.
And don't delay this plan.
And don't tell me your bones are weak.
For I know that you're not sick.

IV

Where no preacher dares to go,
There I'm charged to go.
This is – yes – a lordly ruse
That baits me for abuse.

And this voice must trouble me
To set a doomed race free?
I make haste to cross the river.
But, ah, not to Nineveh.

A haven hides beside the sea.
It will be safe for me.
My plan is flee towards Tarshish.
To reach there is my wish.

And the hour comes for me
To unveil my hidden plan
To sneak aboard a ship and flee
Towards a peaceful land
Where I shall have full release
And live a life of ease
And die – not haunted by a call
To go and seek the lost.

Beside a ship, upon the shore,
There's no one near to see.
I'll sneak away for evermore
To save my heart and soul,
To save my aging heart and soul
From this undue behest.

Now I am aboard a ship.
I've had my flight begun.
I wish for a world of sleep
While my flight may last.

Midway on a tranquil sea
The wild storms slumber on.
May I not exult and say
My luck has just begun!

V

Now cease to fret and furl the sails
And make the anchors sink.
Let's ask the lots to whose misdeed
Our perils trace their link.

Then comb the vessel deck by deck
And sweep the cabins clean.
Yet a stowaway may prove
The agent of our sin.

So what wrong of yours has raised
The storms against our ship
And shares among our guiltless crew
Your stowaway's deserts.

You will go to quell the storms.
Accept the sacrifice.
It's in keeping with our norms,
Not my mere surmise.

VI

What if I accept and die?
Can't you see I fret?
Spare me, I won't tell a lie,
I hate to meet regret.

VII

You confessed to have done some wrong.
Upon your tongue we act.
Be kind to help the rest of us.
We'll lift you if you choose.
And then I think your state is blest,
As so you're not to lose.

VIII

True! The preacher did the wrong
That'd roused the angry storms:
Now he's sinking in the sea
They've all returned to sleep.

IX

There! A man that churns the sea!
Thrashing from above!
Watch out! As he comes to me!
Perhaps a meal for you!

X

I can see my brother whale.
But I burp with food.
If you're not so filled as well,
Then your luck is good!

XI

Another meal is not my wish.
But look round what you see.
If he's such that ruins the sea,
Then his fate is sealed.
But if just a hapless voyager,
Whose luckless vessel sank,
We'll take him straight to Nineveh:
In safety, and to rest.

XII

He holds a book! A man of learning!
Bring him in your gut!
We must rush to Nineveh!
The nearest shore from here!

XIII

Twice the sun has gone to sleep
And risen in our sight.
Here, again, he's wide awake
And bathes the sea in light.
Do I err to fear for him?
The one within your gut:
Trapped beyond his reach of light,
Unseen by day or night.

XIV

Be glad to know he's still alive.
He stirs in every way.
Though as one that yearns, I think,
To see the light of day.

XV

That he may know – and live to tell –
The wonder that I am,
That's spent three days within a whale
And have not come to harm.

XVI

How I wriggle in the gut
Of this commodious whale
With all I dared to scheme, and plot,
And chart with tact, as well.
Will they learn that think their will
Can thwart the voice within?

XVII
The land is now within your reach.
And the moment right!
Go from house to house and preach
My life redeeming light.

XVIII
Master, I arise to go.
I'm your acolyte.
To Ninevites I go to show
Your life redeeming light.

www.ingramcontent.com/pod-product-compliance
Lightning Source LLC
Chambersburg PA
CBHW031153160426
43193CB00008B/346